Willi

by Iain Gray

Lang**Syne**
PUBLISHING
WRITING *to* REMEMBER

LangSyne

PUBLISHING

WRITING *to* REMEMBER

79 Main Street, Newtongrange,
Midlothian EH22 4NA
Tel: 0131 344 0414   Fax: 0845 075 6085
E-mail: info@lang-syne.co.uk
www.langsyneshop.co.uk

Design by Dorothy Meikle
Printed by Printwell Ltd
© Lang Syne Publishers Ltd 2019

ISBN 978-1-85217-426-2

Williamson

MOTTO:
A little by degrees.

CREST:
A sheaf of wheat.

NAME variations include:
Will
Willie
Williams
Wilson
Willson
MacWilliam
MacWilliams
McWilliams

Chapter one:

The origins of the clan system

by Rennie McOwan

The original Scottish clans of the Highlands and the great families of the Lowlands and Borders were gatherings of families, relatives, allies and neighbours for mutual protection against rivals or invaders.

Scotland experienced invasion from the Vikings, the Romans and English armies from the south. The Norman invasion of what is now England also had an influence on land-holding in Scotland. Some of these invaders stayed on and in time became 'Scottish'.

The word clan derives from the Gaelic language term 'clann', meaning children, and it was first used many centuries ago as communities were formed around tribal lands in glens and mountain fastnesses.

The format of clans changed over the centuries, but at its best the chief and his family held the land on behalf of all, like trustees, and the ordinary clansmen and women believed they had a blood relationship with the founder of their clan.

There were two way duties and obligations. An inadequate chief could be deposed and replaced by someone of greater ability.

Clan people had an immense pride in race. Their relationship with the chief was like adult children to a father and they had a real dignity.

The concept of clanship is very old and a more feudal notion of authority gradually crept in.

Pictland, for instance, was divided into seven principalities ruled by feudal leaders who were the strongest and most charismatic leaders of their particular groups.

By the sixth century the 'British' kingdoms of Strathclyde, Lothian and Celtic Dalriada (Argyll) had emerged and Scotland, as one nation, began to take shape in the time of King Kenneth MacAlpin.

Some chiefs claimed descent from ancient kings which may not have been accurate in every case.

By the twelfth and thirteenth centuries the clans and families were more strongly brought under the central control of Scottish monarchs.

Lands were awarded and administered more and more under royal favour, yet the power of the area clan chiefs was still very great.

The long wars to ensure Scotland's

independence against the expansionist ideas of English monarchs extended the influence of some clans and reduced the lands of others.

Those who supported Scotland's greatest king, Robert the Bruce, were awarded the territories of the families who had opposed his claim to the Scottish throne.

In the Scottish Borders country – the notorious Debatable Lands – the great families built up a ferocious reputation for providing warlike men accustomed to raiding into England and occasionally fighting one another.

Chiefs had the power to dispense justice and to confiscate lands and clan warfare produced a society where martial virtues – courage, hardiness, tenacity – were greatly admired.

Gradually the relationship between the clans and the Crown became strained as Scottish monarchs became more orientated to life in the Lowlands and, on occasion, towards England.

The Highland clans spoke a different language, Gaelic, whereas the language of Lowland Scotland and the court was Scots and in more modern times, English.

Highlanders dressed differently, had different

customs, and their wild mountain land sometimes seemed almost foreign to people living in the Lowlands.

It must be emphasised that Gaelic culture was very rich and story-telling, poetry, piping, the clarsach (harp) and other music all flourished and were greatly respected.

Highland culture was different from other parts of Scotland but it was not inferior or less sophisticated.

Central Government, whether in London or Edinburgh, sometimes saw the Gaelic clans as a challenge to their authority and some sent expeditions into the Highlands and west to crush the power of the Lords of the Isles.

Nevertheless, when the eighteenth century Jacobite Risings came along the cause of the Stuarts was mainly supported by Highland clans.

The word Jacobite comes from the Latin for James – Jacobus. The Jacobites wanted to restore the exiled Stuarts to the throne of Britain.

The monarchies of Scotland and England became one in 1603 when King James VI of Scotland (1st of England) gained the English throne after Queen Elizabeth died.

The Union of Parliaments of Scotland and England, the Treaty of Union, took place in 1707.

Some Highland clans, of course, and Lowland families opposed the Jacobites and supported the incoming Hanoverians.

After the Jacobite cause finally went down at Culloden in 1746 a kind of ethnic cleansing took place. The power of the chiefs was curtailed. Tartan and the pipes were banned in law.

Many emigrated, some because they wanted to, some because they were evicted by force. In addition, many Highlanders left for the cities of the south to seek work.

Many of the clan lands became home to sheep and deer shooting estates.

But the warlike traditions of the clans and the great Lowland and Border families lived on, with their descendants fighting bravely for freedom in two world wars.

Remember the men from whence you came, says the Gaelic proverb, and to that could be added the role of many heroic women.

The spirit of the clan, of having roots, whether Highland or Lowland, means much to thousands of people.

Meanwhile, many families proudly boast the heraldic device known as a Coat of Arms, as featured on our front cover.

The central motif of the Coat of Arms would originally have been what was borne on the shield of a warrior to distinguish himself from others on the battlefield.

Not featured on the Coat of Arms, but highlighted on page three, is the family motto and related crest – with the latter frequently different from the central motif.

Clan warfare produced a society where courage and tenacity were greatly admired

Chapter two:

Royal and ancient

Denoting 'son of William', 'Williamson' is ranked at 89 in the list of the 100 most common surnames in Scotland, while it is the third most common surname in England.

Derived from the equally popular forename of William, it has truly warlike connotations, stemming as it does from the Germanic 'will' and 'helmet', as in an armoured helmet worn on the battlefield.

Popularised in England after William the Conqueror's Norman invasion of 1066, its popularity in Scotland is attributable to the mid-twelfth to early thirteenth century reign of the Scots monarch William the Lyon.

The name, however, was already present in Scotland before the advent of either William the Conqueror or William the Lion – a presence that may come as a surprise to bearers of the name today because it has firm roots in ancient and royal Celtic tradition.

This is through the Gaelic name form of Mac *Mhic Uileim*, or MacWilliam, the name designation of a distinguished royal dynasty that was brutally extinguished in the early thirteenth century.

Of the Scottish Royal House of Duncan II and with Badenoch and Lochaber as their main territory, the MacWilliams periodically rose up in revolt, claiming a right to the throne.

But it was during the reign of William the Lion's successor, Alexander II, that their ambitions were finally and bloodily quashed.

By 1229, the sole remaining heir of the MacWilliams was the infant daughter of their Chief, who had been killed in battle, and the medieval *Lanercost Chronicle* relates how she was put to death in a manner considered horrific for even those particularly brutal times.

The *Chronicle* states:

MacWilliam's daughter, who had not long left her mother's womb, innocent as she was, was put to death, in the burgh of Forfar, in view of the market place, after a proclamation by the public crier.

Her head was struck against the column of the market cross, and her brains dashed out.

By such means, Alexander II not only finally crushed the MacWilliam threat to his throne, but also managed to nearly totally expunge their very name from the Scottish historical record.

However, bloodied but unbowed, bearers of the name, in later spelling variations that include Williamson, managed against all odds to not only survive but also in many cases to thrive and make their personal mark on the pages of the vibrant drama that is Scotland's turbulent history.

In addition to their own very personal heritage and traditions that include the motto of 'A little by degrees' and crest of a sheaf of wheat, the Williamsons of today, as a sept, or sub-branch, of Clan Gunn, are also entitled to share in their traditions.

With their main territories in the far north of Scotland, encompassing Sutherland, Caithness and the Orkney Islands, the ancient Clan Gunn claims descent from Sweyn Asleifsson, also colourfully known as The Ultimate Viking.

It is through his grandson, Gunni, that the clan, whose motto is 'In peace, in war' and crest a hand clutching a sword, takes its name – with 'Gunni' an Old Norwegian word indicating 'war' or 'battle'.

The Gunns and their kinsfolk such as the Williamsons, Jamiesons, Robinsons and others were for centuries engaged in vicious clan warfare with their territorial rivals the Keiths.

They met in combat in 1438 at the battle of Blare-tannie, in Caithness.

This was a conflict in which the Keiths, supported by their allies the Mackays, emerged victorious – albeit with great slaughter on both sides.

Twenty-six years later, in 1464, the chiefs of the Gunns and the Keiths agreed to meet at the chapel of St Tears, near Girginhoe, Caithness, in a bid to settle their centuries-old differences.

The agreement was that 'twelve horses from each side', implying that the chiefs would each be accompanied by no more than twelve horsed warriors, should meet for trial by combat.

But an outnumbered Gunn contingent was slaughtered when the Keiths arrived with two men to each of their twelve horses.

The Gunns never forgot this act of treachery and, 70 years later, they exacted a belated revenge by killing George Keith, Chief of the Keiths, and twelve of his clansmen.

In the much more peaceful times of the

1970s, however, representatives of both clans met at St Tears to sign a Bond of Covenant and Friendship.

This was in 1978, symbolically bringing to an end a bitter feud whose roots lay in the dim and very distant past.

As a sept of the Gunns, the Williamsons of today are also entitled to wear their tartan.

The Gunns and their kinsfolk such as the Williamsons were also members of the mighty confederation of clans known as Clan Chattan, which until as late as the eighteenth century was the main power in the Badenoch region of Speyside.

With its motto of 'Touch not the cat without a glove', and crest of a rampant wildcat, Clan Chattan also included within its ranks the Shaws, Mackintoshes, MacPhersons, Farquharsons, MacThomases, McBains, Macleans, McGillivrays and Davidsons.

In Lowland Scotland, one of the most colourful bearers of the Williamson name, in what was otherwise a particularly dark and bloody period of the nation's turbulent history, was the Covenanting Church of Scotland minister David Williamson – renowned in ballad as 'Dainty Davie.'

A National Covenant, pledging defence of the Presbyterian religion, had been signed in the

Greyfriars Kirkyard, Edinburgh, in February of 1638, about eight years after he was born.

Copies were circulated throughout Scotland, and the hundreds of ordinary men and women who subscribed to it, then and later, became known as Covenanters.

Following the restoration to the throne of Charles II in 1660, the death knell for the Covenanting movement was sounded when a Recissory Act was passed, declaring the Covenant illegal.

Episcopal rule was foisted on the Scottish Church, and all ministers who refused to adhere to this new order were deprived of their parishes.

Along with their congregations, many ministers literally took to the hills, preaching at open-air meetings known as conventicles.

Lookouts were posted to keep a wary eye out for the approach of Government troops, known as dragoons, and justice was executed on the spot for those unfortunate enough to fall into their hands.

Constantly persecuted by the forces of authority, the Covenanters rose in futile rebellion in November of 1666 and, as a sign of the harsh treatment that was to be subsequently meted out to them, many of the prisoners taken were tortured and hanged.

A Covenanting victory was achieved at the battle of Drumclog in June of 1679, only to be followed a few short weeks later by resounding defeat at the battle of Bothwell Brig, near Hamilton, by a force commanded by the Duke of Monmouth.

Nearly 800 Covenanters were killed and 1,400 taken prisoner.

Five years before the battle of Drumclog, David Williamson had been minister of St Cuthbert's Church, Edinburgh, but was denounced as a rebel for having held conventicles.

Forfeiting his official ministerial charge, he was allowed to return in 1687 following the granting of reprieves known as Indulgences, but was denounced yet again three years later as a Covenanting rebel.

Pursued by the authorities, he found shelter in the homes of a number of Covenanting sympathisers.

These included the Kerr family of Cherrytrees, near Leith.

As dragoons approached their home, where Williamson had found refuge, Lady Cherrytrees put him in bed dressed in women's nightclothes beside her daughter Jane – passing him off to the dragoons as her daughter's 'bedmate.'

This was a ruse to which Williamson is said to

have 'modestly and readily consented', and while Lady Cherrytrees entertained the unsuspecting dragoons to food and drink, the bold Covenanter took full and lascivious advantage of the situation in which he found himself by getting his 'bedmate' pregnant.

He subsequently married her, making her the second of the eight wives he had before his death in 1706, the father of at least nine children.

His pre-marital escapade with Jane Kerr became the subject of the ballad *Dainty Davie*, one of the many later collected for posterity by Scotland's national bard Robert Burns, and one verse of which reads:

> *When he was chased by a dragoon,*
> *Into my bed he was laid doon,*
> *I thought him worthy o' his room,*
> *And he's aye my Dainty Davie.*

Chapter three:

Chains and slavery

For a nation whose forebears have frequently fought and died in the cause of freedom, it comes as something of a shock to learn that parents once lived in terror of their young sons being kidnapped from their native Scotland and sold into slavery.

It was in 1760 that a 30-year-old man, Peter Williamson, arrived in Scotland from the American colonies with a rather odd and disturbing tale to relate – one that would later provide some of the inspiration for Robert Louis Stevenson's novel *Kidnapped*.

His claim was that he had been kidnapped in Aberdeen and sold into slavery on the American plantations nearly twenty years earlier.

In 1762, after publishing an account of his kidnap and subsequent adventures in America, *French and American Cruelty; exemplified in the life and various vicissitudes of fortune of Peter Williamson*, he raised a civil action against the Burgh of Aberdeen, accusing it of culpability in allowing him to be kidnapped by agents of William Fordyce, an Aberdeen merchant and magistrate.

Williamson was imprisoned for a time in Aberdeen on libel charges, but later won his civil action and £100 in damages.

He had been born in 1730 in the parish of Aboyne, Aberdeenshire, where his father was a tenant farmer.

Aged ten, he was sent to school in Aberdeen, where he lived with an aunt.

His civil action chillingly relates how at that time it was a common and well-known practice among the merchants of Aberdeen and other areas to pick up young, healthy, boys from the streets and surrounding countryside.

They were confined in barns and other convenient out of the way places until such time as a sufficient number of them were gathered.

In what proved to be lucrative 'trade' for the merchants and their associates, they were then packed aboard a vessel to be sold as slaves on the plantations of America or the West Indies.

This was Peter Williamson's heart-rending fate.

His civil action states how "it was the

misfortune of the Pursuer to fall into the hands of one employed by Bailie William Fordyce and Company, merchants in Aberdeen, to pick up boys."

Plucked from the streets along with a number of other young lads, he was held in a building owned by rich merchants before, in July of 1743, being put aboard a vessel bound for America.

Locked below decks, he found himself in the company of 67 other unfortunate boys who had either been taken from the streets or from the surrounding countryside.

The vessel, *Planter*, docked in Philadelphia after a voyage of nearly three months, and where the bewildered lads were sold off to local farmers and merchants.

Bought by a farmer who had also arrived in America from Scotland as a slave but who had been able to regain his freedom, Williamson was fortunate in that he also later managed to secure his freedom.

But he became a victim of the savage battles waged against the Indian and French forces then in the colonies – with the woman he had married being killed and he for a time being held a captive of Delaware Indians.

Following his return to his native land and his ultimately successful action against the Burgh of Aberdeen, he opened a coffee shop in Edinburgh's Parliament House.

He became a well-known figure, fondly known as Indian Peter because of his custom of parading through the city streets colourfully dressed in Native Indian costume.

Responsible for the compilation of Edinburgh's first street directory, he also introduced the Penny Post system to the city.

He died in 1799 and waas laid to rest in Old Calton Cemetery – dressed in his Native Indian costume.

Another Scottish bearer of the Williamson name who lived through rather unusual times in America was John Williamson, a noted political radical who was born in Glasgow.

Immigrating to the United States as a young man, he joined the Communist Party of America in 1922, becoming active in its youth wing, and two years later attending the 4th World Congress of the Young Communist International, in Moscow.

In 1949, during the period of the 'Red Scare'

that swept America, he was among a number of leading American Communists who were arrested and imprisoned.

He was immediately deported to Britain after serving a five-year term in prison.

Becoming a prominent member of the Communist Party of Great Britain, he died in 1974.

In battle, John Leon Williamson, born in 1921 in Ash, North Carolina, was the U.S. Navy Seaman First Class who was posthumously awarded the Navy Cross.

He had survived action, aboard the U.S.S. fighting cruiser *Raleigh*, during the Japanese attack on Pearl Harbor on December 7th, 1941, but was later killed while manning a gun during the assault on Guadalcanal in November of the following year.

It was for this action that he was awarded the Navy Cross, while the U.S. Navy vessel *John L. Williamson* was named in his honour.

Chapter four:

On the world stage

From film and music to sport and literature, bearers of the Williamson name and its equally popular spelling variations, have achieved fame and distinction.

Described by the noted English playwright John Osborne as "the greatest actor since Marlon Brando", **Nicol Williamson** was born in 1938 in the Scottish town of Hamilton, South Lanarkshire.

Despite coming from a humble working class background, he was able to study at the Birmingham School of Speech and Drama, making his first major stage appearance in 1964 in Osborne's *Inadmissible Evidence*, for which he won a Tony Award when the play transferred from the London stage to Broadway.

He later starred in a film version of the play, while other films in which he has starred include the 1968 *The Bofors Gun*, the 1985 *Lord Louis Mountbatten – The Last Victory*, the 1981 *Excalibur* and, from 1996, *The Wind in the Willows*.

Not only a former competitive swimmer but

also a film star, **Esther Williams** was born in 1921 in Inglewood, California.

She first came to the attention of Hollywood film executives while competing in American regional and national swimming contests, and Hollywood put her talents in the pool to use in a number of films of the 1940s and early 1950s known as 'aqua musicals', that featured diving and synchronised swimming.

Born in Toronto in 1989, **Keenan MacWilliam** is the Canadian actress who plays Carole Hanson in the television series *The Saddle Club*, while films in which she has appeared include the 1999 *The Bone Collector*.

A star from 1958 to 1978 of 26 of the popular British *Carry On* films, **Kenneth Williams** was the comic actor of radio and film born in 1926 in Islington, London, while **James Williamson** was the American actor who became Australia's leading theatrical manager.

Born in 1845 in Pennsylvania and becoming established as a comedian with the California Theatre of San Francisco, he settled in Australia in 1872 with his wife, the comedienne Maggie Moore.

Later founding the theatrical management company of J.C. Williamson, after being granted the rights to present Gilbert and Sullivan operas in Australia, he died in 1913.

Born in Melbourne in 1942, **David Williamson** is the contemporary Australian playwright and screenwriter whose play *Don's Party* was adapted for film in 1976.

A collaborator on screenplays that include the 1981 *Gallipoli* and the 1982 *The Year of Living Dangerously*, he was appointed an Officer of the Order of Australia in 1983, while he is also the recipient of an Australian Film Institute (AFI) Award for Best Screenplay for *Gallipoli*.

Also behind the camera lens, **Kevin Williamson** is the American screenwriter, born in 1965 in New Bern, North Carolina, whose credits include the 1996 horror *Scream* and, from 2009, *The Vampire Diaries*.

John Williamson, born in 1881 in Liverpool, and the son of an American sea captain, made an unusual contribution to the world of film in the early years of the twentieth century.

His father, Charles Williamson, had invented a deep-sea tube structure for use in underwater repair and salvage work.

Williamson refined his father's invention in

1912 to create the photosphere – through which, by the addition of illumination and cameras, both still and motion pictures can be taken of the ocean depths; he died in 1966.

Bearers of the name have also excelled, and continue to excel, in the world of music.

Born in 1945 in Quambatook, Victoria, **John Williamson** is the best-selling and award-winning country music singer and songwriter whose song *True Blue*, from his album *Mallee Boy*, has become the anthem for the Australian national cricket team.

An Officer of the Order of Australia, he is also the recipient of two Australian Record Industry Association (ARIA) awards and a number of Golden Guitar Awards from the Country Music Awards of Australia.

From Australia to the United States, **Hank Williams**, born Hiram King Williams in 1923 in Mount Olive, Alabama, was the singer and songwriter widely regarded as one of the most important country music artists of all time.

Responsible for a string of hits that include his 1949 *My Bucket's Got a Hole in It*, *Move it on Over*, *Your Cheatin' Heart* and *Take These Chains from My Heart*, he is an inductee of the Native

American Music Hall of Fame and the Rock and Roll Hall of Fame. Aged only 29, he died on New Year's Day, 1953.

His son, **Hank Williams, Jr**., born in 1949, is also a country singer and songwriter, as is his own son, **Hank Williams III**.

With nicknames that include "The Emperor of Easy", **Andy Williams** is the American singer best known for his 'signature song' of *Moon River*, first released in 1962.

Born in 1927 at Wall Lake, Iowa, and the recipient of 18 gold and three Platinum certified albums, his many other major hits include his 1957 *Lips of Wine* and the 1967 *Can't Take My Eyes off You*.

A co-founder in the early 1960s of the Motown group The Temptations, **Otis Williams** is the American singer with the distinctive baritone voice who was born in 1941 in Texarkana, Texas, while in a different musical genre **John Finlay Williamson** is considered to have been one of the twentieth century's most influential choral conductors.

Born in 1887 in Canton, Ohio, he was the founder, at the Westminster Presbyterian Church of Dayton, Ohio, of the Westminster Choir which later toured the world.

He died in 1964, forty-four years after founding the choir.

Recognised as one of the most prolific composers of film scores in the history of motion pictures, **John Williams** is the American conductor and composer who was born in 1932 in Queens, New York City.

The winner of no less than five Academy Awards, four Golden Globes and seven BAFTA Awards for his scores, his many compositions include the theme for the 1975 *Jaws*, the *Star Wars* saga and the *Indiana Jones* and *Harry Potter* films.

In the highly competitive world of sport, **Corliss Williamson** is the retired professional baseball player who was born in 1973 in Russellville, Arkansas.

An inductee of the Arkansas Sports Hall of Fame, he played during his 12-year National Basketball Association (NBA) career with teams that include the Sacramento Kings, Toronto Raptors, Detroit Pistons and the Philadelphia 76ers.

From baseball to basketball, **John Williamson** was the American player for teams that include the New York Nets and the Washington Bullets; born in 1951 in New Haven, Connecticut, he died in 1996.

On the tennis court, **Venus Williams** and her

younger sister **Serena Williams** are regarded as two of the greatest female players of all time.

Born in 1980 in Lynwood, California, Venus, at the time of writing, has been ranked World No. 1 in singles on three occasions by the Women's Tennis Association, while Serena, born in 1981, has, at the time of writing, been ranked World No. 1 in singles on five occasions.

On the fields of European football, **Bobby Williamson** is the former Scottish striker who played for teams that include Clydebank, Rangers, Kilmarnock and Rotherham United.

Born in Glasgow in 1961, he has also managed teams that include Kilmarnock, Hamilton and Chester City, while he was appointed manager of the Uganda national team in 2008.

In the Canadian national sport of ice hockey, **Mike MacWilliam**, born in 1967 in Burnaby, British Columbia, is the former professional player who played in the National Hockey league (NHL) during the 1995 to 1996 season for the New York Islanders.

Also on the ice, but in this case in the high speed and dangerous "sledging" discipline known as skeleton racing – **Amy Williams** is the English competitor, born in 1982 in Cambridge, who won the silver medal in the event at the 2009 World Championships at Lake Placid and gold at the 2010 Winter Olympics in Vancouver.

On the cricket pitch, **Kane Williamson**, born in 1990 in Tauranga, is the New Zealand Test cricketer who represented his country in the 2011 Cricket World Cup, while in the sport of motor racing, **Roger Williamson** was the British driver who won the 1971 and 1972 British Formula Three Championships.

Born in 1948 in Ashby-de-la Zouch, Leicestershire, he was killed during the 1973 Dutch Grand Prix when a suspected tyre failure caused his car to flip upside down and catch fire.

In the world of science, **Alexander Williamson**, born in London in 1824 of Scottish stock and who died in 1904, was the eminent chemist known for his research on the formation of ether through the interaction of sulphuric acid on alcohol.

Bearers of the name have also been influential in the creative world of the written word – one of the most noted being the English naturalist and writer **Henry Williamson**.

Born in 1895 in London, he is known for social history and nature novels, in particular *Tarka the Otter*, winner of the 1928 Hawthornden Prize for Literature.

Author of a number of other books that include his 1930 *The Patriot's Progress* and the 1972 *The Scandaroon*, he died in 1975.

In contemporary times, **Eric Williamson**, born in 1961 in Sacramento, California, is the American author whose books include his 1999 *East Bay Grease* and the 2009 *Welcome to Oakland*.

In the futuristic realms of science fiction, **John Williamson**, born in 1908 in Bisbee, Arizona Territory is the writer who was hailed as 'the Dean of Science Fiction' following the death in 1988 of fellow science fiction writer Robert A. Heinlein.

The recipient of a World Fantasy Award for Lifetime Achievement twelve years before his death in 2006, his many books include the 1930 *The Green Girl*, the 1955 *Star Bridge*, the 2001 *Terraforming Earth* and the 2006 *The Stonehenge Gate*.

One of the most eccentric bearers of the Williamson name was the English businessman, property owner and philanthropist **Joseph Williamson**, born in 1769 near Barnsley, Yorkshire. Accruing a substantial fortune as a merchant in Liverpool, he subsequently invested much of his wealth in having a series of mysterious tunnels built through the local sandstone near his home in the Edge Hill area of the city.

It has been speculated that the tunnels, built at depths of between 10ft (3m) and 50ft (15m), and in some cases stretching for considerable distances, had been constructed to allow refuge for Williamson and his friends in the event of a natural catastrophe of Biblical proportions.

The likeliest explanation, however, is the one that the philanthropist gave himself – that the tunnels were built to provide much needed employment and a weekly wage to local men.

Despite his wealth, he habitually dressed in untidy and patched clothes, and one of his other eccentricities included once inviting guests to dinner and serving up a humble fair of hard biscuits and porridge.

Many of the guests took offence and promptly left – but those who remained were treated by Williamson as true friends and, accordingly, treated to a lavish feast.

His relationship with his wife appears to have been far from idyllic.

On one occasion he set free all the birds from her aviary, declaring that 'it was a pity that men did not also have wings to enable them to achieve liberty.'

He died in 1840, while several of his tunnels survive today as popular tourist attractions.